Sarah

ROME:
FREE THINGS TO DO
The Freebies and Discounts Travel Guide to Rome

The final guide for free and discounted food, accommodations, museums, sightseeing, outdoor activities, attractions, events, music, theater and rides.

Published by UNITEXTO

UNITEXTO
Digital Publishing

TABLE OF CONTENTS

Brief Introduction to Rome

FREE THINGS TO DO

Churches and Religious Sites
Parks, Gardens and Neighborhoods
Music and Festivals
Attractions
Art and Shows
Museums
Markets
Accommodations
Food & Drinks

DISCOUNTS AVAILABLE

Transportation and Attractions
Museum and Attractions
Food
Hotels
Tours
Shopping

Brief Introduction to Rome

Rome is one of the most culturally rich cities in the world today. Nestled on the banks of River Tiber, Rome witnesses the architectural embrace of the ancient world and the modern world. The city is full of beautiful attractions and sights and people say that even a month's stay is not enough to experience all. You can check out the various guides and mobile apps for the latest on Rome attractions but there is very little information for those who want to enjoy the city on a shoestring budget. Thankfully, there is something for everyone in Rome. We have put together a comprehensive of list of free things to do or see in Rome including discounted tours and attractions.

FREE THINGS TO DO

Churches and Religious Sites

Thing to do: St Peter's Basilica

> *Description:* St Peter's Basilica is the epicenter of Roman Catholicism. It is located in the Vatican City and is open on all days for free tours. The tourists enjoy going to the top of the dome. You can climb all 323 steps to go to the summit but there is small fee for this. The view of the Roman landscape from the top is simply awesome. However, if are not willing to go to the top then you need not pay anything. It is to be borne in mind that since this is an active church with daily Mass services, a stringent dress code is enforced here. The queue here is very long as it is one of the topmost attractions of Rome.
>
> *Cost:* Free
>
> *Location:* Piazza San Pietro
>
> *Date & Time:* daily, 7 am to 6:30 pm

More Information at:

http://www.vatican.va/various/basiliche/san_pietro/index_it.htm

Thing to do: Church of San Luigi dei Francesi

Description: All fans of Caravaggio would love to visit San Luigi dei Francesi. This Navona Church houses works of three of the baroque artists – Calling of St Matthew, Matthew and the Angel & Matthew's Martyrdom. There is absolutely no cost of admission but the Church remains closed during lunch hours (12:30 am to 3:00 pm).

Cost: Free

Location: The Church is in the Navona neighborhood; a short distance away from the Barberini Metro stop.

Date & Time: daily, 10 am to 12:30 pm and 3:00 pm to 6:45 pm

More Information at: http://saintlouis-rome.net/

Thing to do: Church of Sant'lgnazio Di Loyola

Description: The Sant'Ignazio is known for its ethereal ceiling. The visitors to this landmark Church claim that to get the full effect of this beautiful ceiling, you should stand on the disk that is set into the floor of the nave. Free guided tours are available on every Tuesday, Thursdays and Saturdays, 3 to 6 pm.

Cost: Free

Location: Just a few blocks from the Trevi Fountain.

Date & Time: daily, 7:30 am to 7 pm (closed during lunch only).

More Information at:
http://chiese.gesuiti.it/chiesa-di-santignazio/

Thing to do: Basilica di San Clemente

Description: The Basilica di San Clemente is of great interest to those interested in archaeology. It is a 2nd century pagan temple that was found underneath a 4th century church which was again under a 12th century church. Travelers are truly fascinated by this amazing story of the church and they come in droves to absorb

7

the history lesson that it provides. Visitors are requested to ignore the people around the church as they falsely claim to be affiliated with the church and will tell you that you cannot enter unless you give a donation. In reality, though, the church is free to enter. However, you need to pay a small fee to go to the lower levels but it is well worth the cost.

Cost: Free

Location: Via Labicana, near the Colosseo Metro station.

Date & Time: daily, 0900 to 1230 and 1500 to 1800 (closed during lunch only).

More Information at:

http://basilicasanclemente.com/eng/

Thing to do: St Valentine's Skull

Description: The flower-crowned sight of St Valentine is one of the most awe-inspiring sights on this planet. It is located in a gold box and is surrounded by candles and fresh bouquets. The skull is a really intriguing attraction for all visitors including the old Roman temple inside which it is located.

Cost: Free

Location: Piazza della Bocca della Veritas.

Date & Time: daily, 0900 to 1700

More Information at:

http://www.atlasobscura.com/places/st-valentines-skull

Thing to do: Santa Maria Maggiore

Description: Pope Liberius had built this church to the Madonna in memory of a meteorological miracle in AD 356. There have been many extensions and re-buildings but traces of the 13th century mosaics and the marvelous Byzantine 13th century mosaic of Mary still remains. The Sistine and Paoline Chapels were added in the 16th and 17th centuries respectively.

Cost: Free

Location: Piazza Santa Maria Maggiore.

Date & Time: daily, 7am to 6:45pm

More Information at:

http://w2.vatican.va/content/vatican.html

Thing to do: Santa Maria del Popolo

>*Description:* A chapel was built in AD 1099 to steer away the demons of Emperor Nero. There are many reasons to visit this 15th century church but the most compelling one is a mosaic depicting the horoscope designed by Raphael.
>
>*Cost:* Free
>
>*Location:* Nearest stop is Metro Flaminio. From here a bus will take you to Piazza del Popolo.
>
>*Date & Time:* Monday to Saturday, 7am to noon and Sunday, 7:30am to 1:30pm and 4:30pm to 7:30pm
>
>*More Information at:*

http://www.italyguides.it/en/lazio/rome/squares-and-fountains/piazza-del-popolo

10

Parks, Gardens & Neighborhoods

Thing to do: Trastevere

Description: If you want to have a look at real Rome then you must spend at least a couple of hours at Trastevere. This neighborhood is located just south of Vatican City and is home to the Santa Maria, a lot of restaurants and neighborhood shops. Trastevere is at a short distance away from the city center but visitors never mind this distance as it is always nice to explore a quiet neighborhood with cheap food. This place allows you to have a more authentic look at Roman life than any other place in Rome.

Cost: Free

Location: South of Vatican City.

Date & Time: daily, anytime

More Information at:

http://www.lonelyplanet.com/italy/rome/trastevere-and-gianicolo/travel-tips-and-articles/77701

11

Thing to do: Piazza Navona

> *Description:* Piazza Navona is one of the best known public squares in Rome. It's beginning dates back to the end of the 15ᵗʰ century but today the whole square is filled with people sipping coffees, lots of street performers and innumerable shops. There are a few impressive monuments by Bernini and Borromini.
>
> *Cost:* Free
>
> *Location:* Just get down from the metro at Barberini and walk for a mile in the west direction.
>
> *Date & Time:* daily, anytime
>
> *More Information at:*

http://www.turismoroma.it/cosa-fare/piazza-navona

Thing to do: Campo de' Fiori

> *Description:* Everyone should visit Campo de' Fiori at least twice in a trip – once during the day for its market and in the evening for the vibrant nightlife. The character of Campo de'Fiori has not

changed over the years and it looks the same as it did in the early 1800s. But now the place is full of cafes, pizzerias and gelaterias. During the day, you can roam through the bustling markets and shop for fresh veggies and fruits while the bar scene at night attracts a lot of revelers across Rome.

Cost: Free

Location: Piazza de Campo de' Fiori

Date & Time: noon to midnight

More Information at:

http://www.turismoroma.it/cosa-fare/campo-de%E2%80%99-fiori?lang=en

Thing to do: Ancient Appian Way

Description: The Ancient Appian Way has a rich history that dates back to 312 BC and has witnessed historical events such as the execution of the army of Spartacus in 71 BC and the burial of Cecila Metella. These days you can actually stroll along the way and see the monuments that fall in your way. Both foreign tourists and locals have concluded that Appian Way is worth the long trek. You may hire a tour guide as the smallest details along the way can provide a lot of insight. Visitors, however, should come prepared with a good walking shoes and a bottle of water. Always visit this attraction during the day as the area becomes a bit seedy after nightfall.

Cost: Free

Location: Southern Rome. Bus # 118 or 218 can take you there from Metro station

Date & Time: day

More Information at:

https://www.ricksteves.com/watch-read-listen/read/articles/time-travel-on-romes-ancient-appian-way

Music & Festivals

Thing to do: Listen to blues at the Big Mama

Description: The blues joint opened in 1984 and offers free admission to majority of the shows. It is one of the most popular live music venues in the city of Rome. It is a small but cozy venue that can seat 150

people at a time. Apart from the blues, the venue also hosts disco, rock and jazz.

Cost: Free

Location: Vicolo di San Francesco a Ripa

Date & Time: Mon – Sat: 9 pm to 1:30 am, shows start from 10:30 pm

More Information at: www.bigmama.it

Thing to do: Watch the Miracle Players at the Forum

Description: This is an English-language cosmopolitan theater troupe which is recognized by the Italian Ministry of Culture. The plays are funny and original and consist of actors from across the world. The plays deliver a humorous twist to ancient history and beautifully re-enacts the glory and fate of the erstwhile Roman Empire.

Cost: Free

Location: Vicolo di San Francesco a Ripa

Date & Time: Mon – Sat: 9 pm to 1:30 am, shows start from 10:30 pm

15

More Information at: www.bigmama.it

Thing to do: Be in Rome during Estate Romana

> *Description:* Estate Romana is the main summer festival in Rome. The whole city becomes a stage as the festival is dedicated to outdoor performances. Hundreds of film showings, dances and art displays are held during this time and majority of them free admission. One may watch an interesting theater performance among the ruins of Ostia Antica or listen to a blues concert from the steps of a palazzo.
>
> *Cost:* Free
>
> *Location:* throughout Rome
>
> *Date & Time:* daily, throughout the day
>
> *More Information at:*

http://www.estateromana.comune.roma.it/

Attractions

Thing to do: Trevi Fountain

Description: This is a must see attraction on the itinerary of any visitor to Rome. The Trevi Fountain is situated among a dense concentration of shopping places, hotels and the nightlife. It is a great example of baroque design and has a distinctive mythological character. There is a lore that throwing coins into the fountain with the right hand over your left shoulder will guarantee that you will return to Rome, fall ion love with an attractive Roman and will eventually marry him/her. The Trevi Fountain looks beautiful at night when the fountain is fully illuminated.

Cost: Free

Location: The Trevi Fountain is near the Barberini metro stop; Piazza di Trevi

Date & Time: open 24 hours

More Information at:
http://www.turismoroma.it/cosa-fare/2742

Thing to do: Roman Forum

Description: The Roman Forum is not as popular as the Colosseum but visitors say that the Roman Forum is more interesting and free! It consists of some of the most important structures in ancient Rome like shrines, government houses and monuments. Although much of the complex is in ruins, one can easily view the remnants of the Temple of Saturn, the Arch of Septimius Severus and the House of the Vestal Virgins.

Cost: Free

Location: Largo Romolo e Remo

Date & Time: 8:30 am to 4 pm

More Information at:

http://www.turismoroma.it/cosa-fare/fori?lang=it

Thing to do: Pantheon

Description: Raised in 120 AD, the Pantheon is one of the most amazing attractions in Rome. One can pay his respects to Raphael and the Italian kings, Victor Emmanuel II and Umberto I. The Pantheon is located within Piazza della

18

Rotunda and is a perfect setting for a sup of coffee, gelato or a slice of pizza.

Cost: Free

Location: Piazza della Rotunda

Date & Time: daily, 8:30 am to 7:30 pm

More Information at:
http://www.turismoroma.it/cosa-fare/pantheon

Thing to do: Gianicolo Hill

Description: Gianicolo Hill is located just outside the ancient city; so it cannot be counted among the 'Seven Hills' of Rome. It provides one of the most amazing views across the rooftops. The hill also provides a wonderful view of the domes and spires that make up the Roman skyline. The statue of Garibaldi is located on a hilltop and this is easily one of the best spots to enjoy a great view. Everyday at midday a cannon is fired here to maintain the tradition that was started way back in 1847 to signal the time of the surrounding bell towers.

Cost: Free

Location: One can reach the summit of Gianicolo by climbing Trastevere's Via Garibaldi.

Date & Time: any time of the day

More Information at:

http://www.turismoroma.it/quartieri/gianicolo-monteverde?lang=en

Thing to do: Spanish Steps

Description: Any visitor to Rome should climb the alluring Spanish Steps. You can start from Piazza di Spagna and climb up the same stairs that the famous writers Byron and Balzac climbed way back in the 19th century. One will come across the Spanish steps, the Keats Shelley House and lots of shopping options near the Spagna metro stop. There are many tourists who are not really impressed by the Spanish Steps but we recommend that you visit it at least once as it is yet another free attraction. The view from the top of the Spanish Steps is quite impressive.

Cost: Free

Location: Piazza di Spagna

20

Date & Time: any time of the day

More Information at:

http://www.turismoroma.it/cosa-fare/scalinata-di-trinita-dei-monti

Art & Shows

Thing to do: View contemporary art at the Sala 1 Gallery

Description: Sala I opened in 1970 and at that point of time it was the first art gallery to showcase contemporary and experimental art. In 1993 it hosted an exhibition on South African art and even projects from Iraq and Bangladesh. Even today exhibitions are held from time to time and people are encouraged to visit these exhibitions to have a unique experience.

Cost: Free

Location: Piazza di Porta San Giovanni 10

Date & Time: Tue - Sat: 4:30 pm to 7:30 pm

21

More Information at:

http://www.salaimartin.com/component/joomgallery/sala-i-martin/els-matins-162.html

Thing to do: Enjoy a film for free

Description: The Casa Del Cinema in the beautiful Villa Borghese is part of an ambitious project that transformed the pavilion into a hub for the silver screen. The state-of-the-art projection equipment is the most modern in the city making Casa Del Cinema a dreamland for film buffs. From time to time special presentations are arranged where you get to mingle with the stars and directors of the film. Films from the Venice Film Festival are screened here along with original language films.

Cost: Free

Location: Largo Marcello Mastroianni 1

Date & Time: open daily.

More Information at:
www.casadelcinema.it

Museums

Thing to do: Explore the Vatican Museum

> *Description:* Although normally you will require a ticket to enter Vatican Museum, you should enter the museum on the last Sunday of the month as admission is totally free from 9am to 12:30 pm. The museum is one of the most revered gems in the Roman coronet and a must-visit attraction in any Italian tour. One should never miss the chance to explore the inside and outside of this magnificent building. The Sistine Chapel which is housed inside the museum has the nine panels by Michelangelo that accounts for the creation of the cosmos and the man.

> *Cost:* Free

> *Location:* Viale Vaticano

> *Date & Time:* Mon – Sat: 9am to 6pm and Sunday 9am to 12:30 pm (free entry)

> *More Information at:*
http://www.museivaticani.va/

Thing to do: Visit the Historical Museum of the Liberation of Rome

>*Description:* If you are interested in political history, then you should visit this museum on your tour of Rome. This building was the former HQ of the Nazi Commander from 1943 and thereafter it was the cultural office the German Embassy in Rome. The Museum houses memorabilia connected with the struggle against the German vehicles. Some of the major representatives of the Roman Resistance were tortured and murdered here.
>
>*Cost:* Free
>
>*Location:* Via Tasso, 145
>
>*Date & Time:* Mon – Sun: 9:30am to 12:30pm.

More Information at: http://www.viatasso.eu/

Thing to do: Visit the Burcardo Theater Museum

>*Description:* The Burcardo Museum houses an impressive collection dedicated to

24

Italian theater history. The museum is open to the public since 1932 and it has a good collection of costumes, artifacts, beautifully crafted sculptures and a photo archive that has beautiful black and white images of thespians in action.

Cost: Free

Location: Via del Sudario

Date & Time: Tuesday and Thursday – 9:15 am to 4:30 pm and Friday – 9:15 am to 1:15 pm

More Information at: http://www.burcardo.org

Markets

Thing to do: Porta Portese

Description: Porta Portese is a Sunday morning market that you really cannot afford to miss. The vendors here sell everything from books to antiques but the main focus here is on clothes – both new and used. Once you are here you will get a real flea market experience but if you are looking for more authentic goods, then you will have to look elsewhere.

Cost: Free

Location: Via di Porta Portese

Date & Time: any time of the day

More Information at: http://www.portaportese.it/

Thing to do: Find treasures at Monti's Vintage Market

Description: The hip quarter of Monti is located at a short distance from the Colosseum. It hosts a superb 'urban' market every weekend and is held in the conference hall of Grand Hotel Palatino. One can expect to find everything here such as handicrafts, retro clothing, homeware items and furniture. There are independent stores and galleries are located along the small streets of this area.

Cost: Free

Location: Very close to the Colosseum

26

Date & Time: any time of the day

More Information at:
http://www.romeing.it/mercato-monti-borghetto-flaminio/

Accommodations

Thing to do: Find free accommodations through home exchange websites

Description: If you are traveling on a budget you will find that 1/3rd of your allocated budget is being spent on accommodation only. So it will be great if you can stay for free in Rome. But what's the catch? Well, if you are a guest at somebody else's house then at some point of time you should be ready to host your friends when they visit your country. The concept is very popular in this part of the world and it helps you to stay for free in a foreign location.

Cost: Free

Location: Various areas of Rome

Date & Time: any time of the day

More Information at:
http://www.globalfreeloaders.com/

Food & Drinks

Thing to do: Bar hopping for free snacks and canapés during the Happy Hour

> *Description:* There are many bars and cafes in town that give out free snacks to draw patrons. This usually runs in the Happy Hours i.e. between 5pm and 7pm although many bars and cafes start at 7pm and last longer. This practice started in Milan but now it has spread to Rome and other Italian cities.
>
> *Cost:* Free
>
> *Location:* Various areas of Rome
>
> *Date & Time:* usually between 5pm to 7pm
>
> *More Information at:*

http://www.reidsitaly.com/destinations/lazio/rome/dining/aperitivi.html

DISCOUNTS AVAILABLE

Transportation & Attractions

Thing to do: Buy a Roma Pass

> *Description:* The Roma Pass is a travel pass that can drastically reduce the cost of visiting the sights and attractions of Rome. It is available in 2 variants – the EUR 36 pass lasts for 3 days and the EUR 28 pass lasts for 48 hours and does not cover some of the sights outside the city center.
>
> *Discounts available:* The holder of the card is entitled to unlimited rides on all public buses and the Metro, free admission to the first 2 sights that you visit from the list and discounted admission to all other sights. You will also get a sightseeing guidebook and discounts on cultural events.
>
> *How to get the discount:* The card is very easy to use. You can simply show the card and gain entry into the attractions and enjoy free rides on the public transportation system. The card is available for purchase at any museum,

metro stations and Rome tourist info point.

Dates and times: anytime of the day for transport and as per visiting hours of the attractions.

More information at: http://www.romapass.it

Museums & Attractions

Thing to do: Museo Nazionale Romano Cumulative Ticket

Description: The Museo Nazionale Romano is a single admission card which is good for 3 days and is availed at all 4 branches. It is definitely the best sight-seeing card in Rome and is available for a mere EUR 7 to EUR 10.

Discounts available: The holder of the card can gain entry into Palazzo Massimo alle Terme, Palazzo Altemps, Cryptia Balbi and the Baths of Diocletian. The card is a good deal as it affords admission to all the four branches.

How to get the discount: Just show the card and gain entry. The card is available

30

from any participating museum or from its website

Dates and times: as per visiting hours of the sights.

More information at:
http://www.coopculture.it

Thing to do: Archaeologia Card

Description: The archeology card is useful for 7 days from the date of first use. The card costs EUR 23 and you can pick one at the Colosseum. The major downside of this card is that you need to visit practically everything to enjoy the savings. Many experts believe that Roma Pass is a much better option but you can pick one if you think this card is more useful for you.

Discounts available: The archaeology card includes admission to the Roman Forum, the Colosseum, the sites of Roman National Museum, the Palatine Hill, the Tomb of Cecilia Metella and the Baths of Caracalla. The card can be easily purchased from entrance to any of the above attractions or from the Rome Visitor

31

Centre. This card does not any discounts on transportation.

How to get the discount: Just show the card at the entrance to gain entry

Dates and times: As per visiting hours of the attractions.

More information at: http://www.coopculture.it

Food

Thing to do: Stick to local food

Description: It is worth mentioning here that food is one of the main expenses in any trip in any part of the world. If the weather is good, you can always order a pizza for yourself or order pizza by weight. The *paninis* are also excellent and they are quite cheap.

Discounts available: Pizza in Rome normally costs around EUR 7 for a simple *margherita* but prices can go up if you order more exotic varieties of pizza. You can do as the Romans do and order a *fritto misto* before the pizza.

32

How to get the discount: The pizzerias usually opens for dinner i.e. from 8 pm or so. Décor may be spare the food is really high quality. Roman pizzas are generally thin-crusted but they are very filling.

Dates and times: after 8pm; generally for dinner

More information at:

http://www.myromeapartment.com/rome-city-guide/eating-and-drinking/

Hotels

Thing to do: Stay in one of the budget hotels

Description: There are a number of hotels in Rome like THE BEEHIVE   which offers eco-friendly rooms at really cheap rates. The amenities in each room include the supply of organic soaps, linens and shampoos. Some of these hotels have an outdoor garden and arrangements for yoga classes and massage therapy.

Discounts available: Most of the budget or discounted hotels in Rome offer double-bed rooms with shared bathrooms. The minimum rate is EUR 80 and the price includes rate of the room only.

How to get the discount: The discount is available throughout the year. So you can just walk in and request for a room at a discounted rate.

Dates and times: it is available on each day of the year

More information at: http://www.the-beehive.com

Tours

Thing to do: Buy a 48 hour Hop-on Hop-off bus ticket

Description: If you are looking forward to a ride on the Hop-on, Hop-off bus and gain a quick entry to the Colosseum then you should opt for this package. This gives you an option to explore the imperial sites of the Eternal City and visit the Baroque piazzas and palazzos. The bus will allow you to get down at the famous Trevi Fountain and toss a coin and ensure a fast track entry into the Colosseum where you can learn about the life of a gladiator. The Palatine Hill and the Spanish Steps are also included in the bus route.

Discounts available: You can book this package for only USD 53 per person.

How to get the discount: The discount is available throughout the year. The individual gets the opportunity to skip the queue for entering Roman Forum, Colosseum and the Palatine Hill.

Dates and times: it is available throughout the year.

More information at:

http://www.getyourguide.com/rome-l33/super-saver-48-hour-bus-tour-colosseum-ticket-t50719/

Shopping

Thing to do: Designer Discounts

Description: Finding discounts on designer clothing is not a tall ask in Rome as there is a mall in Rome which is fully dedicated to designer clothes with huge discounts. Rome also goes on sale twice a year – January and July. This is also a good time to pick up some really good designer clothes at a whopping 50 - 70% discount.

Discounts available: A minimum of 50% discount is offered during the sale period and at malls like MacArthur Glen Castel Romano.

How to get the discount: There are some stand alone stores in Rome which offer discounts throughout the year. These include Antonella & Fabrizio, Le Grande Firme, Atelier Ritz and Mercatino Michela.

Dates and times: it is available throughout the year.

More information at:

http://www.inromenow.com/site%20temp lates/ShopDesignerDiscount.html

Printed in Great Britain
by Amazon

42042079R00030